ALL VIENNA

Text: EDITORIAL ESCUDO DE ORO, S.A. - BRIGITTE KORVIN.
Photographs: EDITORIAL ESCUDO DE ORO, S.A. - VERLAG GAUKELL
Page 53: Pressefotos des Lipizzaner Museums
Arrangement: BRIGITTE KORVIN.
City Map: FLEISCHMANN & MAIR
Copyright, Printing and Production: © EDITORIAL ESCUDO DE ORO, S.A.
VERLAG GAUKELL, VIENNA
6th Edition - I.S.B.N. 84-378-1636-X Dep. Legal. B. 16214-1999

Editorial Escudo de Oro, S.A.

«Viena, seen from Belvedere». *Painting by Bernardo Bellotto (1759).*

ANCIENT, IMPERIAL VIENNA

Due to its exceptional geographic position, located between the Danube and the Alps, sloping down towards the Wienerwald hills, the capital of Austria, with it dynamic, glorious history, has played an important role in the history of Europe. Vienna soon established itself as the heart of the continent because of its position at the crossroads of the great routes of Western and Eastern Europe. The present-day federal capital, at the same time one of the nine states forming the Federal State of Austria, is both the link between the rest of the country and the Alpine region and with the centre of the Danube region.

Under the Emperor Augustus, the Romans occupied the area from the Eastern Alps to the Danube, in an attempt to defend their territories and to cut off access to the Mediterranean from the invaders from the north, and during the reign of Tiberius the XV legion established the oldest, and strongest, military encampment in Austria, Carnuntum, which was the capital of the region for almost 400 years. The frontier entrenchment of Limes was constructed around

the year 50 AD, in times of the Emperor Claudius and a lateral defence, Vindobona, where auxiliary troops were stationed, was established in what is now the third district of Vienna. Around the year 115 AD, when Trajan was Roman Emperor, Vindabona became the region's main garrison. A period of strife ensued and in 400 AD this fortress was devastated by the Visigoths. Relative peace was not restored until Otto the Great reestablished the Eastern March in 960 AD.

The word *Ostarichi* was first mentioned towards the end of the 10th century in a document signed by Otto III, this document becoming a sort of birth certificate for Austria, historically. In 1137, Vienna was first designated as a city, and in the Regensburg imperial diet of 1156, the Eastern March was raised to the status of Duchy and Vienna, then known as Vienni, was made the capital. The origin of the name Vienni, like that of Vindomina or Vindobona, is unknown. Now a series of sovereigns, Duke Rudolf, Duke Heinrich Jasomirgott and Duke Leopold the Glorious, laid the foundation stones of the Vienna we see today.

When Duke Frederich II fell in battle with the Hungars

in 1246, the House of Babenberg, which had ruled the city for more than 300 years, fell with him, and after the Battle of Dürnkrut, fought between Rudolf I of Hapsburg and Ottokar Przemysl, king of Bohemia, at the end of the 13th century, the Hapsburg dynasty became closely linked with the history of Vienna and of the whole of Austria. In 1521, the decision taken by Ferdinand I to transfer the residence of the emperor of the Holy Roman-Germanic Empire to Vienna was of enormous historical importance. In 1529 and 1683, the walled city of Vienna withstood the sieges laid by Turkish troops. The latter victory was of particular relevance, saving as it did Europe and Western civilisation from destruction.

By virtue of its special characteristic as a state embracing more than one nation, Vienna became a crucible of Eastern and Western cultures. In the 18th century, when its architectural appearance was transformed by the influence of the Baroque style, Vienna's beauty, that of "Glorious" Vienna, knew no rival. Throughout the century, which marked a vital period in the history of the city, such buildings as the elegant Schönbrunn and Belvedere palaces, the Church of Saint Charles and the renowned Gala Room of the National Library were constructed.

After the declaration of war with Napoleon in 1813, and the Quadruple Alliance between Bavaria, Prussia, Russia and Austria, Vienna became the historic seat of the Congress bearing its name, and in which Prince Metternich played an important part in the distribution of modern Europe.

In answer to the modern city's need to expand, the city walls were demolished in the mid-19th century, during the reign of Emperor Franz Josef I, and hence was born the Ring, one of the most impressive and beautiful boulevards to be seen anywhere in the world, along which the most diverse range of architectural styles can be admired. Now one of the most attractive promenades in Europe, the Ring is flanked by fine gardens and sumptuous monuments. Under the auspices of Modernism (Jugendstil), the capital underwent enormous expansion in the second half of the last century, witnessing the growth of the modern city, in great contrast with the ancient city and with the Vienna of the Baroque period. Present-day Vienna is an impressive ensemble of contrasting districts, each with its wealth of monuments.

Emperor Franz Josef I died during the First World War, and with him the Hapsburg dynasty was extinguished. The first Republic was proclaimed in 1918 and Austria was annexed by Hitler's Germany in 1938. Ten more years were to elapse after liberation in 1945 before Vienna became once more the capital of a free Austria.

The huge Roman ashlar.

Saint Stephen's Cathedral.

Stephansdom, kanzel. ▷

The most important work of art in the main nave is the magnificent pulpit in late Gothic style by the master-builder Anton Pilgram (photo, above left), from the early XVIth century. The four sides of the pulpit, built from seven blocks of sandstone, show the Latin church fathers St. Augustine, Pope Gregory I, St. Jerome and St. Ambrose. The lizards and toads climbing the staircase symbolize Evil, held at bay by a barking dog (symbol of Good) at the top of the bannister. As with the ''Orgelfuss'', Master Pilgram did not refrain from including a self-portrait on the pulpit (known as the ''watcher at the window''; photo on the left.

Saint Stephen's Cathedral (1, Stephensplatz)

Situated in the world-famous historic centre of the city, in the south-east corner of the old Roman fortress, Saint Stephen's Cathedral stands at the geographic centre of Vienna. The plans which gave the cathedral its basic form were drawn up under the patronage of Duke Rudolf IV, though their author is unknown. The foundation stone of its Flamboyant Gothic nave was laid in 1359, and in 1433 work on the south tower began, to be finished in around 1433 by Hans von Prachatitz, whilst the central body, the work of Hans Puchsbaum, was not completed until 1455. In 1467, Hans von Prachatitz began the north tower, of which only the lower half was finished. From 1511 onwards, no work of significance was carried out on it. The unfinished tower's Renaissance dome was built between 1556 and 1570. The 137-metre high Gothic belltower is a distinctive symbol of the city, surmounted by two more towers known as the ''Pagans'', each 64 metres high. On entry into the main aisle of the cathedral, 110 metres in length, one can see how the building is divided into three sections by twelve columns. The colossal size and tremendous unity of this masterpiece of Gothic religious architecture is overwhelming. In the left-hand nave, over the great altarpiece of the ''Altar of the New Citizens of Vienna'' (Wiener Neustädteraltar), the initials A.E.I.O.U. appear, magnificently carved in wood. These correspond to Frederick III's motto: his tomb is to be found in the right-hand nave. Over the tomb, a splendid carving by the medieval sculptor N.G. von Leiden, is a statue of the emperor with his imperial symbols. Another interesting tomb in the cathedral is that of Prince Eugene of Savoy. The high altar is particularly remarkable, presided over by a statue of the stoning of Saint Stephen, by Tobias Bock.

Saint Stephen's also boasts a fine pulpit, constructed in 1510 by Anton Pilgram, another of the cathedral master-builders, whose magnificent self-portrait, depicted looking out of a half-open window, is to be seen on one of the supporting pillars of the organ. The 14th-century statue of ''Our Lady of Domestic Service'' (Dienstbotenmadonna), as she is known, is also the work of Pilgram.

A platform next to the ''Pummerin'' Bell, another characteristic symbol of the city of Vienna, reached by a lift, offers superb panoramic views of the city and the foothills of the Alps with their beautiful woods.

The cathedral was seriously damaged during the Russian attack of 6 April 1945, which ended with the capture of the city on 13 April. Before this, on 12 March, a devastating air raid by North American bombers had caused considerable destruction to the Sacristy, situated in the east wing, and on 8 April the houses in front of the main entrance were destroyed by fire caused by a fierce Soviet air attack. When Soviet troops entered Vienna on 10 April, retreating German soldiers shelled the city, smashing holes in the cathedral roof in several places. Fire took hold of the building, raging ever more strongly throughout the next two days. The situation was all the more hopeless since the German army had taken the Vienna fire-brigade with them when they left. The effects of the fire were most strongly felt in the north tower. The bells' wooden framework collapsed into the nave, setting fire to the whole of the interior, including one of the ''Pagan'' towers. The dome over the choir-stalls and the main bell came crashing down. On 13 April, the fire's destructive work was completed, much of the vaulting over the central chancel and that of the south wing collapsing and the emperors' oratories and the priceless Gothic choirstalls of the chancel being destroyed. The people of Vienna looked on in desperation and anguish at the destruction of the monument which had been the most constant symbol of the city's past grandeur.

The Viennese people, however, did not resign themselves to merely conserving the image of the cathedral in their memory: they resolved to rebuild it. ''Thanks to the generosity of the Viennese and to the anonymous, patient work of architects and stonemasons'', wrote Otto Stradal, ''The sanctuary has been completely restored, and has assumed once more its original appearance''.

Only the marvellous stained glass windows could not be recreated in the work of returning Saint Stephen's Cathedral to its beautiful former architectural structure.

Der Albertinische chor von süden.

Saint Stephen's Cathedral. The high altar.

Our Lady of Domestic Service.

Altar of the New Citizens of Vienna.

Tomb of Emperor Frederick III.

The «Pummerin» Bell of the north tower.

Finally, also worth a visit are the crypts, falsely known as the Catacombs, which are located beneath the Albertine choir (where, among others, the sarcophagus of the Emperor Rudolf I, the Founder, can be seen). The view from the top of the South Tower is magnificent. The North Tower houses the largest bell in Austria, the ''Pummerin'', weighing 20 metric tons, which is only rung on special occasions (such as New Year's Day). The enormous bell fell onto the nave during a devastating fire in the cathedral on the final day of World War II. It was hung in place again after a seven-year reconstruction effort.

The «Virgin of the Protecting Mantle» (1450-1500).

18th-century statue of Christ.

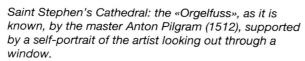

Saint Stephen's Cathedral: the «Orgelfuss», as it is known, by the master Anton Pilgram (1512), supported by a self-portrait of the artist looking out through a window.

Capistrano's pulpit.

*Saint
Stephen's
cathedral.*

Vienna. St. Stephen's
cathedral in 1912
with the South
Tower, the two
Towers of the
"Pagans" and the
Great Gate.
Watercolour by
Franz Kopallik.

View of the inside
of the cathedral.

Saint
Stephen's
Cathedral:
interior.

The «HAAS-HOUSE», built by the well-known architect Hans Hollein (completed in 1990).

ON HOUSE (1., Stock-im-Eisen-Platz 6, Stephansplatz)

The new commercial headquarters were built from 1985 to 1990 according to plans prepared by Hans Hollein.

The first Haas house was located at the same site and became a magnificent warehouse for the Philipp Haas & Sons company. It was built between 1865 and 1867 according to plans designed by August Siccardsburg and Eduard van der Nüll. It was the first warehouse in Vienna built with iron pillars, but was covered with a heavy stone facade on the outside in accordance with current building regulations.

In 1945, it was demolished and replaced by a new building by Carl Appel, Max Fellerer and Eugen Wřle, which was in turn demolished and replaced by Hollein's project. Because of its great round structure with archways, partially covered by glass, it acts as a link between Grabenstrasse and Stephansplatz. The corner of Grabenstrasse and Kärntnerstrasse is the site of the most famous wooden tree trunk in Vienna, the "Stock im Eisen" ("iron stick"). It has been famous since the XVIth century. It is a larch-fir trunk, the remains of a forest that once reached this point. The iron chain that surrounds it has a lock that is impossible to open. There are numerous legends about the (supposedly) 3,000 nails driven into the tree. One study carried out at the beginning of this century revealed that the wood was definitely from a fir tree and that the lock was just a trick.

GRABEN (1. Bezirk)

Graben is, with Kohlmarkt and Kärntnerstrasse, one of the most elegant shopping streets of the city. Its name comes originally from the trenches — "Festungsgraben" in German — which existed here

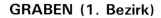

The «Stock im Eisen».

The Column of the Plague in Grabenstrasse.

from Roman times until the second half of the 12th century, and which formed the western limits of the city. The trenches were filled in as part of the expansion of the city which took place under Leopold VI, the Glorious, in 1225, and houses were built in their place. Soon, Graben became a bustling street given over to commerce, with a food market and, from 1702, tombolas and stalls for other games of chance and shops selling gold and silver plate. Since the reign of Maria Theresa, Graben has been the centre of city life. Graben is dominated by the Column of the Plague, dedicated to the Holy Trinity and erected at the command of Leopold I to give thanks for the end of the devastating plague of 1679. Among the artists contributing to the completion of this work were Burnacini and Rauchmiller, but Johann Bernhard Fischer von Erlach was responsible for the central idea of the column, though work had already started on the construction when he intervened. Von Erlach also sculptured the bas-relief of the pedestal. The two fountains situated on either side of the column were designed by Johann Martin Fischer in 1804. One depicts Saint Joseph bowing to one of the children holding the family tree whilst the other, the Saint Leopold Fountain, shows the Babenbergs' patron saint, Leopold III. A niche at the corner of Graben and Kärntnerstrasse holds a log, known as the ''Iron Stick'' (Stock im Eisen), studded with hundreds of nails. It is said that it is the masterpiece of a locksmith, achieved with the help of the devil. When the smith perished, victim of his bargain, all the locksmiths and blacksmiths passing by the site had to hammer a nail into the trunk and say a prayer for the unhappy wretch.

Vienna in 1900. The Grabenstrasse with the Column of the Plague and Leopold Fountain. Watercolour by K.W. Zajicek.

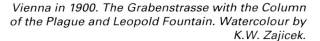

SAINT PETER'S CHURCH (1, Petersplatz)

The second-oldest church in Vienna, founded, according to legend, by Charlemagne. This venerable building was conserved thanks to the financial contributions of the doctor, map-maker and historian, Wolfgang Lazius, in 1555, and of Franziska, Countess of Palffy, in 1643. Restoration began in 1702, following the plans of Lukas von Hildebrandt, work being finally completed in 1733.

St. Peter's Church, Franz Xavev Schleich.

THE CLOCK (ANKERUHR) (1, Hoher Markt)

Between the Anker insurance company building (Hoher Markt 10) and the house at number 10, is the "Ankeruhr", built according to the Modernist plans of the painter Franz von Matsch. Daily at noon, the figures of the clock appear, parading to the rhythms of the music played by the clock.

*The Clock
(Ankeruhr).*

The figures are: Marcus Aurelius; the Emperor Charlemagne; Duke Leopold VI with his wife Theodora von Byzanz; Walter von der Vogelweide; King Rudolf von Habsburg with his wife Anna von Hohenberg; Master-builder Hans Puchsbaum; Maximilian I; Johannes Andreas von Liebenberg; Count Ernst Rüdiger von Starnberg; Prince Eugene of Savoy; Maria Theresa with her husband the Emperor Franz I von Lothringen; Joseph Haydn.

FOUNTAIN OF THE NEWLYWEDS (1, Hoher Markt)

In Vienna's oldest square, **Hoher Markt,** is the Fountain of the **Newlyweds,** also known as the Fountain of Joseph. In 1702, Emperor Leopold I promised to build a fountain in honour of Saint Joseph if his son, Joseph I, returned unhurt from a military campaign. The first version was made in wood from drawings by Johann Bernhard Fischer von Erlach. Shortly after, when this began to show signs of disrepair, Emperor Charles VI commissioned Josef Emanuel Fischer von Erlach to build a new fountain, which was completed between 1729 and 1732, and portrays the marriage of Joseph and Mary.

THE ENTICING SHOPS OF VIENNA

Shopping in Vienna is one of the many delights offered by the city. In the centre, Kärnerstrasse, Graben and Kohlmarkt, this latter a pedestrian area, offer constant enticement to the passer-by, for it is here that most fashionable shops of Vienna, with their dazzling windows, are to be found. There are also many boutiques, fascinating galleries and tiny bazaars scattered among the charming little streets of the old part of the city, where the temptation to stop and buy may be overwhelming. Antique-lovers will be captivated by the Second-Hand Market and the "Flohmarkt", once the state pawnshop, where important art and antique auctions are held. Viennese handicrafts, too, are an attractive demonstration of the taste and skill of the artisans of Vienna. Most popular among these products are Augarten china pieces, handmade dolls, artistically-made ceramic objects and other products made by these craftsmen in wrought iron, enamel and leather, as well as jewellery.

Fashion in Vienna has a long tradition which has justly earned it great fame, and the *haute couture* of Vienna has few rivals. The city boasts an eminent fashion school, situated in the Hetzendorf Palace. "Viennese-style" furniture is also highly appreciated and is produced today in designs faithful to the original models.

A view of Saint Stephen's Cathedral from Kärntnerstrasse.

Various aspects of Kärntnerstrasse.

State Opera House: interior.

THE STATE OPERA HOUSE (1, Opernring 2)

The State Opera, formerly the Court Opera, is to this day one of the foremost opera houses in the world. It was built between 1861 and 1869 to the plans of August von Siccardsburg, who designed the overall structure, and Eduard van der Null, who designed the interior of the building, which followed the historical Florentine-French early Renaissance style. The opera house was inaugurated in 1869 with Mozart's *Don Giovanni,* and the two architects were so strongly criticised that they did not long outlive the opening night. Van der Null committed suicide and Siccardsburg died of a heart attack two months later. The style in which the opera house had been built pleased neither the common people nor the court, and this fact, together with the satiric poem dedicated by the people of Vienna to the bad taste of the architects, were perhaps the cause of their tragic deaths.

The opera house was hit by bombs on 12 March 1945 and only the balcony, foyer, the main staircase and a tea-room survived the resulting blaze. The building was restored, with few changes to its original appearance, between 1948 and 1955 by Erich Boltenstern, Otto Possinger and Zeno Kossak and in 1955 the house adjoining the Ring opened its doors once more with a performance of Beethoven's *Fidelius*, conducted by Karl Böhm.

The greatness of Viennese operatic art springs from its permanent opera company, which counts numerous stars acclaimed all over the world among its members, and, above all, from the brilliance of its orchestra, which, strengthened by members of the Vienna Philarmonic, places the music played at this theatre in a category of its own. Great musicians have conducted here; Gustav Mahler, Richard Strauss, Franz Schalk, Clemens Krauss, Herbert von Karjan and Karl Böhm have all contributed their genius to the artistic splendour of the State Opera House.

The opera house has an area of 9,000 square metres and holds 2,209 spectators. The orchestra pit accommodates 110 musicians, and there are two halls for ballet rehearsals and three for the opera singers, a stage for rehearsals, ten rooms for soloists, an organ room and a studio for radio broadcasts with facilities for up to fifty microphones. There are also nine relays for television broadcasting, and the electricity consumption of the opera house is equivalent to that of a town of 30,000 inhabitants.

Views of the front and interior of the State Opera House.

The Vienna Opera dancers.

THE CAPUCHINS' CHURCH AND THE TOMB OF THE EMPEROR (1, Neuer Markt)

The Capuchins' Church, endowed by the Empress Ana, wife to the Emperor Matthias, who died in 1618, was finished after her death, between 1622 and 1623, and restored according to the original plans in 1936. Built to the precepts of the Mendicant Orders, it is a sober, plain building of little artistic significance. Its importance as a monument is derived from the Tomb of the Emperor or Capuchins' Tomb, the Habsburg family shrine, which contains 138 metal coffins, including those of twelve German and Austrian emperors and fifteen empresses. Only two emperors of the house of Emperor Matthias are not buried here, Ferdinand II, buried at Graz, and in whose reign the first tomb was built and the last Austrian emperor, Charles I, buried in Madeira. The tombs are a record of changing spirit and artistic evolution over three centuries, from the splendour of the times of Maria Theresa or the sombre style of Josef II, to the renewed monumental grandeur of the second half of the 19th century.

Church of the Capuchins.

Crypt of the Capuchins. Tomb of the Emperor Ferdinand I.

Crypt of the Capuchins. Tomb of the Emperor Franz Josef I.

THE FOUNTAIN OF PROVIDENCE
(1, Neuer Markt)

This was built in 1739 by Georg Raphael Donner at royal command. The Empress Maria Theresa ordered the original nude figures, made of lead, to be demolished and they were later substituted for bronze copies. The originals are kept in Lower Belvedere.

THE ALBERTINA MUSEUM
(1, Augustinerstrasse)

This is one of Vienna's most important museums. The building, originally the Silva-Taroucca Palace, dates back to 1781, and was enlarged, incorporating part of the adjoining Augustine monastery, between 1801 and 1804 by Luis de Montoyer, commissioned by the father of Archduke Albert I, Archduke Karl, who defeated Napoleon at Aspern. In 1822, the interior was adapted in classical style by Josef Kornhäusl. Rebuilding after 1945 gave the palace its present form, with the addition of its great outside stairway.

Since 1795, this palace, the residence at that time of Archduchess Maria Cristina and her husband, the architect Albert of Saxony-Teschen, has housed the world-renowned collection of drawings and engravings accumulated by them.

A fundamental part of the museum's treasures is formed by the collection of Prince Eugene of Savoy. The collection of 40,000 drawings and over a million prints, engravings, etchings and lithographs is the largest in the world, as well as one of the most important, and is being continually added to. All the nations and artistic schools in the world are represented here, notably the German schools of the 16th century, including drawings by Dürer, Hans Holbein, Jörg

A typical house of old Vienna, near to Neuer Markt.

Danubios - Brunnen.

Breu, Lukas Cranach, Peter Altdorfer and many more. The Dutch school is represented by Pieter Breughel, Lukas van Falkenborch and Anton van Dyck, the Italian masters by Raphael, Michelangelo, Leonardo da Vinci, Tintoretto, Veronese, Guardi and Canaletto. As limitations of available space make it impossible to exhibit all the works in the collection simultaneously, the works on show are changed every year.

FOUNTAIN OF THE DANUBE (1., Albertinaplatz).

The Albertinarampe fountain was inaugurated on December 24, 1869. The with Carrara marble sculptures are the work of Johann Meixner. The architectural concept based on three bodies was the idea of Moritz von Löhr. Financing was from city funds.
In 1989 the fountain was restored to its orginal appearance.

MONUMENT AGAINST INJUSTICE, FASCISM AND WAR (20., Höchstädtplatz)

This monument, designed by F. Weber, was inaugurated in May 1989 in front of the building of the Central Committee of the KPÖ (Austrian Communist Party). The bronze figure represent of Marsias II by slain after being defeated by Apollo in a music contest. Hrdlicka modified the model, turning the wood god upside-down, thereby suggesting the essence of what it means to be physically at the mercy of someone.

Monument against Injustice, Fascism and War.

*Fine Arts Museum
and the monument
to Maria Theresa.*

THE FINE ARTS MUSEUM (1, Burgring)

One of the most attractive aspects of Vienna is its wealth of important museums, and among these the Fine Arts Museum ("Kunsthistorisches Museum") is outstanding. This museum is also situtated on the Ring, and its exhibits, to be seen in the main building, comprise splendid art collections, some of which, such as the paintings exhibited on the first floor, the plastic arts and crafts to be found on the left-hand side of the mezzanine, the sculpture collection on the right and the coin collection on the second floor, are considered to be among the finest in the world.

The main building consists of 91 exhibition rooms of varying sizes. A complete tour would constitute a walk of four kilometres. The collections include art treasures from Vienna, Graz, Brussels, Prague and Innsbruck. The beginnings of the accumulation of the Hapsburg collection date back to the end of the 13th century, forming the base of Emperor Ferdinand I's important collection, which he bequeathed to his sons, Emperor Maximilian, Duke Ferdinand of the Tyrol and Archduke Karl of Steiermark. Emperor Rudolf II added to his own collection, which he brought to Vienna from Prague, to that of Emperor Ferdinand of the Tyrol. Before this, however, in 1667, the emperial collection was enrichened by the addition of the Gallery of the Dutch Archduke Leopold Wilhelm, städholder in the Netherlands, and during the reign of Maria Theresa, in 1765, the Graz treasure was merged with that of Vienna. In 1889, the collections were united in the building they now occupy. Through purchasing, donations and excavations, the museum's collection grew until it possessed 480,000 pieces, so many that some had to be transferred to another building.

Probably the most valuable collection in the museum, by virtue of its unity, is that of works by the Dutch painter Pieter Breughel, the Fine Arts Museum boasting the most complete collection of his work in the world. Also outstanding are great pictures such as van Dyck's *Samson and Delilah,* a large, Baroque-inspired canvas, Titian's *Diana and Calixtus,* Dürer's

Pieter
Breughel,
Wedding
Feast.
*Fine Arts
Museum.*

Anton
Van Dyck,
Samson and
Delilah. *Fine
Arts
Museum.*

*Fine Arts
Museum:
interior.*

Pieter Paul Rubens, The Fur Coat. *Fine Arts Museum.*

Adoration of the Holy Trinity, Velazquez's *Portrait of the Infanta Margarita Teresa* and three pictures by Rubens, *Portrait of Hélène Fourment, Lamentation for the Dead Christ* and, above all, *The Fur Coat,* a painting on wood of regular dimensions, which he painted in 1638 and which represents a nude woman, her body shining with pearly light, her back and thighs covered by a fur coat. This is a work of daring sensuality revealing the expressive genius of this famous painter of the Flemish school.

The gallery also exhibits masterpieces by Raphael, Rembrandt, van Eyck, Lukas Cranach and many others, but the other sections of the museum are just as interesting: the oriental and Egyptian collection, the antique collection, those of plastic arts and crafts, of medals, coins and monetary units, of antique musical instruments, of arms and the Museum of Austrian Culture. A visit to the Vienna Fine Arts Museum is a delight for the eyes and the spirit. The collections, tastefully exhibited in all the rooms, stir the spirit of the visitor with admiration, and taken altogether give an idea of the importance of Vienna in the cultural life of Europe. It has been justly affirmed that Austria has more masterpieces, both in the field of painting and of sculpture, in relation to its actual geographic size, than any country in the world, with the exception of the Vatican. A tour of the museum's rooms not only stimulates the sensitivity but also encourages the visitor to give free reign to the imagination, permitting him or her to relive the past through the magic of these works of art which reveal both the spirit of a country with a vocation for cultivating artistic creation of all kinds and its desire to conserve and protect such an artistic treasure-trove. Nobody would deny that Vienna is the capital of music, but it is also one of those cities which most value painting and sculpture as an expression of cultural advance and evolution.

Fine Arts Museum: Egyptian art.

Albrecth Dürer, Adoration of the Holy Trinity. *Fine Arts Museum.*

Titian, Diana and Calixtus. *Fine Arts Museum.*

Pieter Breughel, The Tower of Babel. *Fine Arts Museum.*

A room in the Natural History Museum.

THE NATURAL HISTORY MUSEUM
(1, Burgring)

Opposite the Fine Arts Museum is the Natural History Museum, which was also built by Gottfried Semper and Carl V. Hasenauer between 1871 and 1891, its exterior architecture similar in style to that of the former. The museum houses one of the largest natural science collections in Europe, with sections covering mineralology, botany, paleontology, zoology and prehistory.

Natural History Museum.

THE PALACE OF FAIRS (7, Messeplatz)

Formerly the court stables, the building was begun by J.B. Fischer von Erlach in 1719 and was restored and completed in 1721 and 1723 by J.E. Fischer von Erlach. In the centre of this complex was formerly the palace of the court groom.

Church of Saint Michael.

THE IMPERIAL PALACE (1, Bezirk)

Its splendid architecture makes Michealerplatz one of most attractive sights of Vienna. The Church of Saint Michael stands here, formerly the court parish church, a fine 18th-century building containing a magnificent 14th-century chancel.

The square is dominated by the majestic front of the ''Hofburg'', a sumptuous building which was once the imperial palace. In the centre of the façade is a forged iron gate flanked by four groups of sculptures, which immediately draws the visitor's attention. There is an arched niche in each of the two wings containing two fountains symbolising ''The Power of the Earth'' and ''The Power of the Sea''. A great dome crowns the central body of the building, to the left of which the entrance to the celebrated imperial quarters is to be found. These are comprised of a huge audience chamber, a dining-room, where the table has been kept exactly as it was at the time of the Congress of Vienna, when Tzar Alexander occupied this part of the palace, and the rooms of Emperor Franz Josef and Empress Elisabeth, rooms which still evoke the atmosphere in which the couple lived during their years of happiness. These were followed by unhappy times, during which their son committed suicide and the Empress was assassinated. The architecture of the quarters is of noble proportions and is decorated with precious paintings. Nevertheless, it seems that Franz Josef was a man of simple, conventional tastes. He lived with a soldier's austerity and thought of himself as the Austro-Hungarian Empire's first civil servant and officer. Visitors are now shown as a curiosity the balcony from which, behind curtains, the Emperor observed the changing of the guard, watch in hand. Crossing the rotunda of the dome, one reaches an interior square within the palace, in the centre of which is a large monument to Emperor Franz I. The four corners of this square represent the architecture

Kohlmarkt.

Hofbourg.

of four different periods, the oldest being the Swiss Gate, notable for its colours. This gate was built between 1536 and 1552, during the reign of Ferdinand I, and is the most important of the few Renaissance works to be found in Vienna. The mechanism by which the drawbridge was lowered and raised and part of the moat can still be seen here. The gate leads to the Swiss Court and the 15th-century Palace Chapel, of which only the chancel is visible from outside. On Sunday mornings, at 9.30 mass, the famous **Child Singers,** accompanied by the **Vienna Philarmonic Orchestra,** perform masterpieces of religious music in one of the most beautiful and moving spectacles offered by the city.

Imperial Palace: the Swiss Gate.

Saint Michael's Square: entrance to the Imperial Palace.

Inner court of the Imperial Palace and the statue of Emperor Franz I.

The Child Singers of Vienna.

Swiss Gate, the entrance to the chapel and to the museum of treasures.

An extraordinary museum stands opposite the chapel. The richly decorated rooms of this museum exhibit a collection of masterpieces of gold and silver work and jewellery of incalculable value, a veritable treasure-chest to dazzle the visitor. Unique in the world, this museum is divided into two sections, one room for holy treasure, the other for secular works. Specially interesting are the coronation insignia of the emperors of the Holy Roman-Germanic Empire, what was once Maximilian's Burgundy treasure, the jewels once belonging to Maria Theresa, the robes, adorned with precious stones, in which Emperor Franz Josef I was baptised, the superb tunics of the Order of the Golden Fleece, the crown, enlaid with precious stones, worn by the emperors of Austria from the time of Redbeard up to the reign of Franz I, the coronation robes, the golden rose of Maria Theresa, the nail from the Cross, brought back to Vienna during

Imperial Chancellory
wing: the passageway
to Saint Michael's
Square.

«The Power of the
Sea».

«The Power of the
Earth».

The coronation mantle.

Museum of Treasures: the Crown of the Hapsburgs, the imperial orb and sceptre.

Franz Josef I's bedroom.

A view of the interior of the Imperial Palace, with the «Imperial Altarpiece of the Almighty».

Habsburg Monarchs of Austria

Rudolf I (1218-1291), 1276-1282
Albert I (ca. 1250-1308), 1282-1298
Rudolf III (1281-1307), 1298-1306
Frederick I the Fair (1286-1330), 1306-1330
Albert V (II) (1397-1439) (1404) 1411-1439
Frederick V (III) (1415-1493), 1439-1490

Maximilian I (1459-1519), 1490-1519
Charles V (1500-1558), 1519-1521
Ferdinand I (1503-1564), 1521-1564
Maximilian II (1527-1576), 1564-1576
Rudolf II (1552-1612)
Matthias (1557-1619)

Ferdinand II (1578-1637), 1619-1637
Ferdinand III (1608-1657), 1637-1657
Leopold I (1640-1705), 1657-1705
Josef I (1678-1711), 1705-1711
Charles VI (1685-1740), 1711-1740
Maria Theresa (1717-1780), 1740-1780

Josef II (1741-1790), 1765-1790
Leopold II (1747-1792), 1790-1792
Franz II (1768-1835), 1792-1835
Ferdinand I (1793-1875), 1835-1848
Franz Josef I (1830-1916), 1848-1916
Charles I (1887-1922) 1916-1918

the Crusades, and an infinity of cloths encrusted with pearls and gold-embroidered dresses. Also splendid are the reliquaries and other pieces which make up the holy treasure, such as the Cradle of the King of Rome.

Returning to the interior court of this extraordinary palace, we can pause to admire the other three gates. Opposite the Swiss Gate is the Amalia Palace, in early Baroque style. This was begun in 1575 under Emperor Maximilian and was completed in 1611, in the reign of Emperor Rudolf. On the west side of the palace we find the Leopold I wing, built by him between 1660 and 1666 and restored from 1668 to 1670 after it was damaged by fire. The main side of the square is formed by a wing in late Baroque style, which accommodates the Royal Chancellory, built between 1723 and 1730 by Johann Lukas von Hildebrand and Josef Emanuel Fischer, commissioned by Karl V.

A passageway in the Leopold Wing leads to the Square of the Heroes (Heldenplatz), in which stand two equestrian statues, one of which represents the

Imperial Palace: Meetings Chamber.

Monument to Prince Eugene.

Prince of Savoy, who commanded the Austrian troops defending Vienna from the attacks of the Turks. The other is of Archduke Karl, who led the resistance against Napoleonic invasion. This part of the palace, known as New Hofburg, forms a wide semi-circle overlooking the Heldenplatz and the attractive groves of the Volksgarten, one of the loveliest parks of Vienna. Here, history joins hands with art and the imagination conjures up the splendid past of the imperial city.

The Leopold Wing, where the Empress Maria Theresa once had her rooms, is now the official residence of the president of the Austrian Republic. Her prime ministers all resided in the white Baroque building which stands opposite, and this is now the seat of the Federal Chancellory.

Ballroom.

Imperial Palace: the chapel.

The New Imperial Palace.

Equestrian statue of Archduke Karl, with the Volksgarten and the Town Hall in the background.

Statue in honour of Empress Elisabeth.

Imperial Volksgarten: Temple of Theseus.

The Presidential Chancellory.

Seat of the Federal
Chancellory and of
the Ministry of
Foreign Affairs
(1, Ballhausplatz).

The stables at
Stallburg.

Van Gogh, The Antwerp Plain. *Neue Galerie in der Stallburg.*

THE IMPERIAL PALACE STABLES

Building on these -conceived at first as an imperial residence for Archduke Maximilian and later remodelled- began in 1558. The courtyard, which is lined with poplars, is in Renaissance style, and was originally built as stables for the horses of the royal coaches and the riding school. It now houses the Spanish Riding School, and since 1967 the second floor has been used as the new gallery of the Fine Arts Museum.

Van Gogh, Self-Portrait. *Neue Galerie in der Stallburg.*

*Corps de Logis
(Ethnological Museum).*

*Ethnological Museum.
Aztec feather ornament,
early XVIth century.*

Former room for court silver service and tableware; plate decorated with a scene. Vienna porcelain factory, 1804.

Former room for court silver service and tableware; decorated plate. Vienna porcelain factory, 1815.

Former room for court silver service and tableware; floral plate. Vienna porcelain factory, 1820.

DIE HOFBURG IN WIEN

Baualtersstufen
- Mittelalter
- 16. Jahrhundert
- 17. Jahrhundert
- 18. Jahrhundert
- 1. Hälfte 19. Jahrhundert
- ab 2. Hälfte 19. Jahrhundert

LE PALAIS IMPERIAL DE VIENNE

Périodes de construction
- Moyen-Age
- XVIème siècle
- XVIIème siècle
- XVIIIème siècle
- 1ère moitié du XIXème siècle
- à partir de la 2ème moitié du XIXème siècle

IL PALAZZO IMPERIALE DI VIENNA

Epoche di costruzione
- Medioevo
- '500
- '600
- '700
- Prima metà dell''800
- A partire dalla seconda metà dell''800

THE IMPERIAL PALACE OF VIENNA

Periods of construction
- Middle Ages
- 16th century
- 17th century
- 18th century
- first half of the 19th century
- second half of the 19th century

PALACIO IMPERIAL DE VIENA

Periodos de construcción
- Edad Media
- Siglo XVI
- Siglo XVII
- Siglo XVIII
- 1.ª mitad del siglo XIX
- 2.ª mitad del siglo XIX

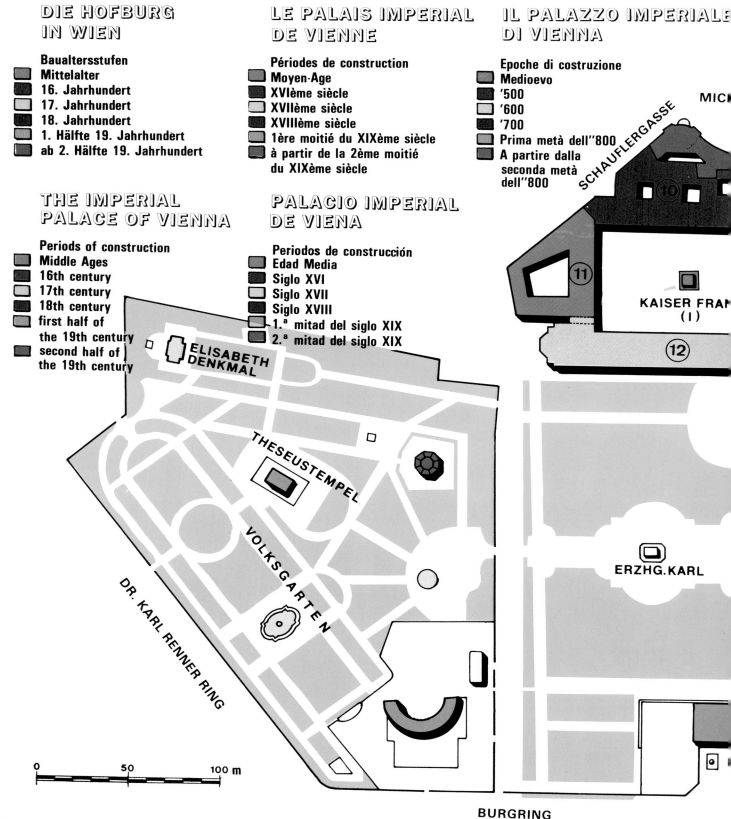

SCHAUFLERGASSE

MIC

10

11

KAISER FRAN
(I)

12

ELISABETH DENKMAL

THESEUSTEMPEL

VOLKSGARTEN

DR. KARL RENNER RING

ERZHG. KARL

0   50   100 m

BURGRING

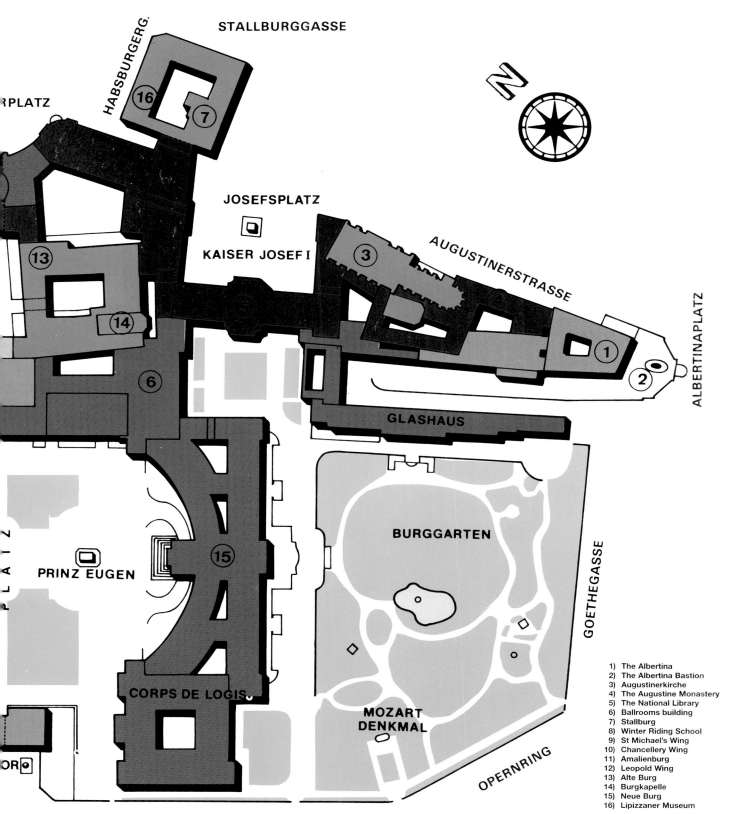

STALLBURGGASSE

HABSBURGERG.

⑯ ⑦

JOSEFSPLATZ

KAISER JOSEF I

AUGUSTINERSTRASSE

③

④

⑬

⑭

⑤

①

②

⑥

ALBERTINAPLATZ

GLASHAUS

BURGGARTEN

PRINZ EUGEN

⑮

GOETHEGASSE

CORPS DE LOGIS.

MOZART
DENKMAL

OPERNRING

1) The Albertina
2) The Albertina Bastion
3) Augustinerkirche
4) The Augustine Monastery
5) The National Library
6) Ballrooms building
7) Stallburg
8) Winter Riding School
9) St Michael's Wing
10) Chancellery Wing
11) Amalienburg
12) Leopold Wing
13) Alte Burg
14) Burgkapelle
15) Neue Burg
16) Lipizzaner Museum

BURGRING

51

Former
room for
court silver
service and
tableware;
Biennais,
gilded
silver
service,
Paris, 1809.
Detail.

Johann Georg von Hamilton (1672-1737). Neput, a dapple-gray, at the gallop, around 1720. Press photographs from the Lipizano Museum.

Spanish Riding School. Uniform, two-cornered hat, riding saddle, whip. © Photograph: Henrie F. Brabec D'Ipra. Press photographs from the Lipizano Museum.

Anonymous painter. Lipizza Imperial Stables. Early 18th century. Vienna Museum of Fine Art. Press photographs from the Lipizano Museum.

Johann Georg von Hamilton (1672-1737). White horse from Karst, around 1720. Vienna Museum of Fine Art. Press photographs from the Lipizano Museum.

THE LIPIZANO MUSEUM

The museum is housed on three floors of the former court pharmacy at the Imperial Palace Stables (1st district, Reitschulgasse 2). It looks back at the history of the Lipizzan stallions, and features graceful portraits, riders' uniforms dating from the Hapsburg monarchy, and fascinating facts from the world of *haute école*. The highlight of the museum is a glimpse at the horses' stables through a soundproof observation window. The shop sells not only equine souvenirs, but also tickets for morning training sessions at the Riding School. Open 9 a.m. to 6 p.m. daily.

Bridle from the gala harness for a team of eight horses from the royal stables, used traditionally by Emperor Francis Joseph at Corpus Christi. Made from gilt brass. Vienna Museum of Fine Art. Press photographs from the Lipizano Museum.

«Pricking the Moor» is an exercise which demostrates the skill of the horsemen, consisting of hitting two wooden heads representing Moors with pistol or lance. Picture by Ignaz Duvivier (1780).

THE SPANISH RIDING SCHOOL (1, Hofburg)

Continuing from Michaelerplatz towards the Opera House, one reaches the Court of Vienna Riding School (Reitschule), where are to be found the Habsburgs's famous stables, with their Lipizzaners from Court of Spain Ridding School. Construction began in 1728 to the plans of Fischer von Erlach and were finished by his son in 1735. The building was used as a winter riding school, and has a gallery supported by 16 Corinthian columns. The Spanish Riding School, founded by Karl VI, is the only one in the world where classical horsemanship is practised. The Spanish horse, a breed of Spanish and Arabic blood, was introduced to Austria in 1580, when the first specimens were brought to Lipizza, now part of Jugoslavia. The movements of the ''Emperor's white horses'', as they are known to this day, are a splendid sight to behold, and the spectacle of classical horsemanship offered by the white studs and their riders constitute a colourful cameo of old, imperial Vienna. The white chargers, gold thread gleaming in their mane, are mounted by horsemen wearing traditional imperial costume; brown coats with black silk cuffs, white leather trousers, high, shining patent

The Director of the Spanish Riding School, Brigadier-General Kurt Albrecht, and his assistants. From left to right: Trainer Steinriegler, Head Trainer Eichinger, Trainer in reserve Bachinger, Head Trainer Kottas, First Head Trainer Lauscha, Brigadier-General Albrecht, Commander Helmberger, Head Trainer Tschautscher, Trainer Krzisch, Trainer Riegler and Trainer Rouland.

Entrance of the trained cuadrilla. Colonel Hans Handler, who was in charge of the riders of the Spanish Riding School, on his horse Siglavy Bona. Colonel Handler worked at the Spanish Riding School from 1942 to 1944 and, following a brief interruption, joined the school again from 1947 to 955. In 1965 he was named Director of the nstitution. He died in the saddle in 1974.

Imperial Palace: staircase, music room and armoury.

leather boots, two-cornered hats with golden cockade and Spanish daggers. Lit by the shimmering chandeliers of the gallery, chargers and horsemen begin their exhibition, composed of elegant prancing and extraordinarily fine skipping movements, reminiscent of the tapping heels of the best Spanish dancers. Then, at a certain moment, these superb beasts begin to dance with awesome elegance, while an orchestra plays minuets, polkas or slow waltzes. Near to the riding school is Josef II Square **(Josefsplatz),** in which stands an equestrian statue of this emperor. The square is surrounded by various Baroque buildings of great beauty, among which outstanding is the **National Library,** built in 1723 by Fischer von Erlach the Younger, following the original plans drawn up by his father, and which conserves collections of enormous value.

National Library: collection of orbs.

National Library.

Saint Joseph's Square:
monument to Emperor
Josef II.

Burggarten: Friedrich Ohmann palm grove (1900).

Burggarten: monument to Mozart.

Burggarten: monument to Emperor Franz Josef I.

The Parliament building, with the statue of Pallas Athene.

PARLIAMENT (1, Dr.-Karl-Renner-Ring)

The Parliament building was constructed between 1874 and 1883 in Greek Revival style to the plans of Theophile Hansen. The centre of the pediment shows the granting of the Constitution by Franz Josef I. On the ramp there are several statues representing Greek and Roman sages, with four horse-breakers at the end, modelled in bronze by Lax. Opposite the Parliament is the Monumental Fountain, built in 1902 by Kundmann, and which depicts the Greek goddess Pallas Athene.

THE TOWN HALL (1, Rathausplatz)

The town hall, in Neo-Gothic style with Renaissance elements, was built between 1872 and 1883 by the architect Friedrich Schmidt. The tower rises to a height of almost 100 metres and is crowned by a figure in copper weighing 3.6 tons representing a State Mercenary with his armour and standard. This figure is referred to popularly by the people of Vienna as ''The Town Hall Man''.

The Vienna Town Hall building serves as the majestic scene for the opening and closing ceremonies of the Vienna holiday week, which takes place in June and constitutes the most important cultural event of the whole year.

Monument to K. Seitz, mayor from 1923 to 1934, in the Park of the Town Hall.

Park of the Town Hall: Monument to T. Körner, mayor of Vienna from 1945 to 1951 and President of the Republic from 1951 to 1957.

Sessions chamber of the Town Hall.

National Theatre.

THE BURGTHEATER
(1, Dr.-Karl-Lueger-Ring)

The Vienna Burgtheater, popularly abbreviated to "The Burg", is one of the oldest, most traditional stages in the world and is also the most celebrated of all the theatres of the German-speaking world. It was first situated in Michaelerplatz, opening, with the permission of Maria Theresa, in 1741 in a former ball room of the emperor's residence, being transferred to its present home in 1888. The Burgtheater was designed by G. Semper and K. Hasenauer. Under such famous directors as Josef Schreyvogel and Heinrich Laube, the theatre soon took its place as the most important stage of the German-speaking world. Statues in the façades of the building pay homage to celebrated poets associated with the history of this theatre and to outstanding theatre personalities. The theatre was completely destroyed by fire in 1945 and was rebuilt between 1951 and 1955, regaining its imposing architectural structure.

National
Theatre:
main
staircase.

The university and the monument to Liebenberg.

THE UNIVERSITY
(1, Dr.-Karl-Lueger-Ring)

The University of Vienna —*Alma Mater Rudolfina*— was founded in 1365 by Rudolf IV and built in Italian Renaissance style by Heinrich Ferstel from 1873 to 1883. It is the oldest university of the German-speaking world.

Opposite this building is the monument to the popular mayor of the city, Johann Andreas von Liebenberg, who acted with great heroism during the second Turkish siege of 1683. Not far from here is the well-known ''House of the Three Maidens'' (Dreimädlerhaus), a typical early 19th-century bourgeois house.

«Dreimäderlhaus».

The Votive Church.

OUTSTANDING RELIGIOUS AND SECULAR MONUMENTS

In addition to the palaces and sculptures which we have already mentioned, the capital of Austria also offers visitors to its squares and streets the chance to contemplate the charm of its many churches, including the **Votive Church** (Votivkirche), which Archduke Maximilian, later to become the ill-fated Emperor of Mexico, ordered built to commemorate the failed attempt on the life of Franz Josef in 1853. The church was built on the scene of the attempted assassination between 1856 and 1879 by Heinrich von Ferstel, and is considered Vienna's most important Neo-Gothic work. The outside walls are of limestone and feature 78 paintings on glass by Geyerling, which decorate the windows. The subtle architectural elements of the building, constructed according to the canons of 13th and 14th century French Gothic style, can best be appreciated at night, when the church is illuminated by artificial lighting. The flying buttress by the chancel is achieves a particularly spectacular effect.

The **Schottenkirche** and the **Schottenkirch** Monastery (1, Freyung) were founded in 1155 by Duke Heinrich II Jasomirgott of the House of Babenberg. Its present form, an early Baroque style, dates back to 1643, when restoration began, being completed in 1648. In place of the Gothic transept, Josef Kornhäusl constructed a convent between 1826 and 1832.

The **"Am Hof" Church** ("former Jesuit Church", 1, Am hof) where Emperor Franz II declared his renounciation of German Imperial dignity in 1806, was built in Gothic style between the years 1386 and 1403. In 1662, after fire had destroyed the interior of the building at the beginning of the 17th century, its beautiful front was rebuilt in Baroque style.

«Maria am Gestade».

Greek Church.

Imperial Church.

The church of Saint-Rupert.

«*Maria am Gestade*».

The existence of the **Church of Maria am Gestade** (1, Salvatory asse) is first mentioned in 1158. After the destruction of the original Romanesque building in 1262, the church was rebuilt, taking on the form it now has, in the 14th and 15th centuries.

The **Church of Saint Rupert** (1, Ruprechtsplatz) is the oldest religious building still standing in Vienna, and was founded in 740, though documents proving its existence date back only to 1161. It has undergone successive reformations throughout its history.

The **Greek Church** (1, Fleischmarkt, 13) was built to the plans of Peter Mollner between the years 1782 and 1887 and was reconstructed in Byzantine style according to the plans of Theophil Hansen between 1858 and 1861.

The centre of Vienna also contains a number of secular buildings of outstanding interest, whether due to their architectural or historic value or to the fact that they number among the typical buildings of this charming city. Mention must be made here

The Kinsky House.

The Pallavicini House.

Civil Arsenal.

The Ferstel House.

«Griechenbeisel» Restaurant.

of the Greek Tavern (Griechenbeisel), one of the oldest and most attractive of the Greek restaurants of the Fleischmarkt, or the many Viennese cafés, symbols of a romantic, splendid Vienna of bygone times, those of the popular master of the waltz, Johann Strauss.

The **Kinsky House** (1, Freyung 4), formerly Daun House, was built between 1713 and 1716 by Johann Lukas von Hildebrandt.

The **Pallavicini House** (1, Josefsplatz 5) was built as the Fries House by Ferdinand von Hohenberg between 1783 and 1784.

The Stock Market.

Hotel Sacher.

«Griensteidi» Café.

«Zum weissen
Rauchfangkehrer»
Restaurant.

A scene in a Vienna café.

Also interesting is the **Ferstel House** (1, Herrengasse 14), named after its architect, Heinrich von Ferstel, built between 1856 and 1880, now the **Central Café.**

The **Civil Arsenal** (1, Am Hof 10), now the headquarters of the fire brigade, was rebuilt between 1731 and 1732 by Anton Ospel.

The **Stock Exchange** (1, Schottenring 16) was built in Neo-Renaissance style between 1871 and 1877 by Theophil Hansen. A fire in 1956 completely destroyed the interior of the building, which was reopened in 1959 after restoration work had been carried out.

THE OLD TOWN HALL (1, Wipplingerstrasse 8) was substituted in its functions by the new town hall built in the Ring in 1883.

The building underwent successive reforms between the 15th century and the beginning of the 18th. There is a lovely interior court, in which stands the "Fountain of Andromeda" by Georg Raphael Donner, constructed in 1741, and a Barque front dating back to 1700.

The old Town Hall.

THE IMPERIAL CHANCELLORY OF BOHEMIA (1, Judenplatz 11), now the seat of the Constitutional and Administrative Tribunal, was constructed between 1708 and 1714 by Johann Bernhard Fischer von Erlach and extended by Mathias Gerl from 1750 to 1754. Bomb damage was repaired between 1945 and 1951. The front by Fischer von Erlach which looks onto Wipplinger Street has been conserved.

The Liechtenstein House.

THE VIENNA CLOCK MUSEUM (1, Sculhof 2) is housed in the former Obizzi House, a 16th-century building, later altered to take on a Baroque style. It contains a huge collection of more than 3,000 pieces of great historic and artistic value.

THE LIECHENSTEIN HOUSE (9, Fürstengasse 2) is a fine Baroque palace now housing the Modern Art Museum. Work on the central building began in 1691 and was completed in 1704 under the architect Domenico Martinelli. The annex was constructed between 1705 and 1711.

◁ *The Vienna clok Museum.*

THE CITY PARK (1, Bezirk)

This park was designed in an English style by the landscape gardener Rudolf Sieböck in 1862, after the course of the river had been regularised. Due to its location in the central area of Vienna, it is a park much visited by tourists and by the Viennese people themselves as an ideal spot for a refreshing stroll in the fresh air.

The most important monument in the park is that dedicated to the memory of the master of the waltz, **Johann Strauss,** though there are also monuments to Schubert, Bruckner, Lehár and Robert Stolz. The **Kursalon** is a popular rendezvous for lovers of the waltz, who meet here to dance to the melodies of this evocative music.

The statue of Franz Schubert.

Modernist staircase and promenade by F. Ohmann (1906).

Kursalon.

Monument to Franz Lehár.

Belvedere Palace.

BELVEDERE PALACE
**(Upper Belvedere 3, Prinz-Eugene 27.
Upper Belvedere 3, Rennweg 6)**

This Baroque palace was built between 1700 and 1725 by the architect Johann Lukas as the summer residence of Prince Eugene of Savoy, commander-in-chief of the Imperial army which defeated the Turks in 1697. Belvedere consists, in fact, of two beautiful palaces, ''Upper Belvedere'' and ''Lower Belvedere''. The magnificent gardens separating the two were designed by Dominque Girard. **''Upper Belvedere''** was used to hold receptions in the time of Prince Eugene, and now houses the **Gallery of the 19th and 20th Centuries,** which has rooms dedicated to classical art, to the Biedermeier style, to the Ringstrasse epoch and to modernism, besides containing important collections of the works of such famous artists as Klimt, Schiele, Kokoschka, Hausner and Hundertwasser.

It was ''**Lower Belvedere**'' which was the Prince's true summer residence. This building now houses the **Austrian Baroque Museum,** which contains sculpture and painting dating back to the 17th and 18th centuries, and in the Orangerie is to be found the **Austrian Museum of Medieval Art,** which exhibits works dating back to the 12th to 16th centuries. In 1945, towards the end of the Second World War, both palaces were severely damaged, but they were subsequently restored with great fidelity to the original plans.
On 15 May 1955, the Great Marble Chamber of ''Upper Belvedere'' was the scene for the signing of the **Treaty of Austria** between the allied, occupying nations, and with this Austria recovered independence and declared its status as a neutral country.

Upper Belvedere: magnificent staircase.

Upper Belvedere: Great Marble Chamber.

Belvedere Palace.

Upper Belvedere:
Terrena Room.

Lower Belvedere.

Lower Belvedere: golden cabinet with Th Apotheosis of
Prince Eugene in marble by B. Permoser.

A panoramic view from Belvedere Palace.

Gustav Klimt, The Kiss.

Illuminated Fountains, with the monument to the Red Fleet in teh background.

THE ILLUMINATED FOUNTAINS
(Schwarzenbergplatz)

To commemorate the first canalisation of the water which had flooded the city in 1873, the fountains of Vienna were built. They were converted into illuminated fountains in 1906.

THE PHILARMONIC SOCIETY CONCERT HALL
(1, Dumbastrasse 3)

This was built by Theophil von Hansen between 1867 and 1870 for the ''Society of Friends of Music''. Every year, the New Year's Eve Concert of the Vienna Philarmonic is broadcast all over the world by television and radio from the Great Hall, or ''Golden Salon''. The building also houses the Conservatory, as well as a permanent exhibition of items illustrating the history of music, scores and a collection of musical instruments from different periods.

The sumptuous «Golden Room», whose acoustics have made it world-famous.

Johann Strauss the Younger
(*25. 10.1825 - 3.6.1899), who was born and died in Vienna.

Ludwig van *Beethoven.
(*December 1770 in Bonn, died 26.3.1827 in Vienna.

Saint Charles' Church:
the altar and pulpit.

Saint Charles' Church:
the organ.

THE CHURCH OF SAINT CHARLES
(4, Karlsplatz)

This is one of the most beautiful Baroque churches in Vienna, and is dedicated to Saint Charles Borromeo. In 1713, when the city was scourged by an epidemic of plague for the seventh time in its history, Emperor Karl VI ordered a church built in honour of the Patron Saint of the Plague. When, in 1716, the plague had been quickly eradicated, Johann Bernhard Fischer von Erlach began to build the Church of Saint Charles, a task which was finally completed by his son Josef Emanuel in 1737.

The church, with its massive, solid dome measuring 72 metres, is, after the Church of Saint Stephen, the most important in Vienna. The front which faces towards the centre of the city is flanked by two Doric columns, 47 metres high, which stand out on either side of the building, crowned by beacons. They are copies of the columns of those built by Trajan and Marcus Aurelius in Rome, and on their pedestals are bas-reliefs representing the life, miracles and death of Saint Charles Borromeo. Notable inside the church is the altarpiece depicting Christ announcing to the Roman centurion that his slave has been cured, a work by Daniel Gran, and the frescoes of the dome, by Johann Michael Rottmayr.

Saint Charles' Church: partial view of the fresco in the dome, The Arrival in Heaven of Saint Charles.

The Modernist «Am Steinhoff» Church, San Leopoldo,
built between 1905 and 1907 by Otto Wagner, and the
church of the psychiatric clinic of Vienna.

Decoration of golden medallions by Kolo Moser (6, Linke
Wienzeile 40).
«Majolica House», decorated with a mosaic by Wagner,
who financed the whole work, including plant and flower
decorations on the front.

The Modernist building known as The Secession, by Josef Maria Olbrich (1897-1898, 1, Friedrichstrasse 12).

Faculties of the Technical University and the university library (4, Karlsplatz, 4, Wiedner Hauptstrasse).

The old Modernist railway station by Otto Wagner in Saint Charles' Square.

MODERNISM IN VIENNA

The words ''Modernism'', **Jugendstil** in German, ''modern style'' in English and ''art nouveau'' in French, all have their origin in the title of the Munich magazine ''Jugend''. In the German-speaking countries, the word signifies the style which became dominant in most of Europe at the end of the 19th century and the beginning of the 20th. In Spain, for instance, the work of the great Modernist architect Gaudí was outstanding. In Vienna, Modernism took the form of a kind of revival of the Baroque style, continuing a deeply-rooted tradition in this city, joined with elements taken from the Romantic movement, the mixture resulting in an exhuberant decorative style in which symbols from the world of plants and flowers and curved and ondulating forms predominate.

Among the Modernist artists active in Vienna, outstanding were **Josef Hoffmann, Gustav Klimt, Josef Maria Olbrich** and **Otto Wagner,** founders of the ''Austrian Association of Plastic Artists'' (1897). Between 1897 and 1898, Olbrich constructed the building known as ''The Secession'', a centre for this group of artists, which also contains exhibition and club facilities. The building has a cubist form, crowned by a dome of gold and iron laurels. Though destroyed in 1945, it was rebuilt in 1969.

THE "NASCHMARKT" (6, Linke Wienzeile)

The "Naschmarkt" dates back to 1774 and has been, since 1819, a fruit and vegetable market. One of its most picturesque elements is provided every Saturday by the lively, bustling "Flea Market" (Flohmarkt), where second-hand bargains can be bought in the open air. Goods of all types are on offer here, ranging from a rickety chair to paintings, drawings, lamps, furniture of all kinds, even genuine antiques.

Papageno Gate.

AN DER WIEN THEATRE
(6, Linke Wienzeile 6)

Supposedly to the plans of Franz Jäger, this theatre was built between 1798 and 1801, commissioned by the librettist of Mozart's "The Magic Flute", Emanuel Schikaneder, and soon became one of the most popular theatres in Vienna. Works by Beethoven and Mozart were performed here, and Johann Nestroy achieved triumphant success in this theatre. When "Gold and Silver" operetta was popular, names like Millöcker, Strausss, Zeller, Eysler, Kálmán and Lehár featured prominently in the programmes of the An Der Wien, and the theatre is even today considered to be one of the most important concert halls in Europe.

«An der Wien» Theatre: main curtain with decorations from «The Magic Flute».

Wolfgang Amadeus Mozart, 27-1-1756, Salzburg - ✝5-12-1791, Vienna.

The Artistic House by Hundertwasser.

Hundertwasser's combustion fountain.

THE ARTISTIC HOUSE OF VIENNA - WHAT A MUSEUM SHOULD BE. Among the old clay houses of Vienna there arose a new cultural symbol: a forum for international exhibits, a home for Hundertwasser's work, a museum where one feels at home, an atypical house, a modern adventure, a voyage to the land of creative architecture, a melody for eyes and feet.

THE HUNDERTWASSER HOUSE (3, Löwengasse) is a municipal building designed by the well-known Viennese painter Friedensreich Hundertwasser, constructed by the city council between 1983 and 1985. In accordance with his principles as an ecologist, the artist renounced the use of plastic materials in the architectural structure, using only bricks and large quantities of wood in the construction. The greeness of the horizontal surfaces and the bright colouring of the front which characterise the house have made the building an important tourist attraction in the city.

Details of Hundertwasser's house.

THE PRATER (2 Bezirk)

Formerly the hunting grounds of the emperor and the nobility, this is an area covering 1,300 hectares. In 1766, Emperor Franz II opened the Prater to the general public. The broad stretches of grass and the marvellous landscape make this park a favourite haunt of walkers and, especially, sportsmen, horse-riders, runners, cyclists and the like. Facilities here include the famous stadium, the equestrian events venues, a modern swimming-pool and many other sports areas.

In 1537, a chestnut tree-lined avenue, now the main avenue of the Prater, was created by order of Ferdinand II. This leads from the star to the band-stand, formerly the hunting pavilion. The big wheel of the ''Wurstelprater'', the traditional Viennese fairground, was constructed between 1896 and 1897 by the English engineer Walter Basset to coincide with the 1897 Universal Exhibition. It has a height of 64.75 metres and weighs around 430 tons. All the carriages on the big wheel were burnt and the operating system destroyed in 1945 during the last few days of the Second World War, but soon the wheel was turning on its steel axis once more, albeit with only half the original number of carriages.

Next to the big wheel is the **Lilliput Train,** a miniature railway which takes passengers on a delightful four kilometre return journey through the lovely fields of the Prater, right up as far as the stadium.

The Big Wheel at the Prater. ▷

◁ *Prater.*

TECHNICAL MUSEUM
(14, Mariahilferstrasse 212)

This was built between 1909 and 1913 by Hans Schneider and opened in 1918, when the interesting exhibitions relating to the history of technical progress had been assembled. These include Watt's steam engine, dating back to 1790, Mitterhofer's typewriter (1864), Josef Maderspergers' sewing machine (1815) and the first petrol-driven automobile, built by Siegfried Marcus in 1875. Another section devoted to the **Railway Museum** exhibits historic locomotives and antique railway carriages.

Technical Museum.

Schönbrunn Palace.

SCHÖNBRUNN
(13, Schönbrunner-Scholossstrasse)

One of the most characteristic monuments of the city of Vienna. Some 300 years ago, the area now occupied by the park of the Schönbrunn Palace was covered by thick woods sheltering abundant game. Documents dating back to 1311 reveal that the Katter Windmill once stood here and, in 1471, the tiny Katter Castle was built next to it.

The property was acquired by Maximilian II in 1568, and he ordered the buildings converted into hunting pavilions and established a zoo on the site. During a hunt in 1619, Emperor Matthias discovered the beautiful "**Schönner Brunnen**" fountain, and the waters of this spring supplied the palace, to which it also gave its name, until the end of the 18th century. After the destruction of the palace at the hands of the Turks, a new building was designed between 1692 and 1693 by Johann Bernhard Fischer, commissioned by Leopold I. This was a grand new building, intended to surpass the splendours of the Palace of Versailles, and was to have been built on what is now the Gloriette Hill (Gloriettehügell). Finally, however, in 1700, a much more modest building was practically completed, to which Emperor Josef I loved to make long visits.

Josef's son, Karl VI, neglected construction work, which was finally completed by Maria Theresa, under whose reign the palace took on its definitive form. The construction of the castle was finished by first Nicolas Pacassi then by Valgamini, and the park was given a French design between 1705 and 1706 by Jean Trehet, but their present aspect is due to the

work of Ferdinand von Hohenberg and Adrian van Steckhoven between 1753 and 1775. Since the time of Maria Theresa, Schöbrunn was the favourite residence, after the Hofburg, or Imperial Palace, first of the Roman-German emperors, then of the emperors of Austria. A total of 1,441 rooms and chambers provided accommodation for the court, of which 390 were given over to living quarters and official court functions. There were 139 kitchens serving more than 1,000 people in this building which, covering 1.76 square kilometres, was four times larger than the Vatican.

In 1814 and 1815, during the Congress of Vienna, the Schönbrunn was the scene of dazzling receptions. Napoleon's only son, the Duke of Reichstadt, lived and died here, and he who was to become Emperor Franz Josef I was born in this palace in 1830, dying in the same place in 1916. Emperor Karl I declared his abdication at Schönbrunn in 1918. During the Second World War, the buildings received the impact of 270 bombs, which caused severe damage to them. From 1945 to 1947, the castle was the headquarters of the British army of occupation, and restoration work on the damaged buildings was completed in 1952, the luxurious chambers being now used for diplomatic receptions.

In the magnificent Schönbrunn park, with an area of 197 hectares, the principal monuments are the Fountain of Neptune, the Obelisk and the Roman Ruins. The flowery gardens stretch as far as the summit of a hill, on which stands the **Gloriette,** an open colonnade 19 metres in height and 95 in length, flanked by Roman trophies, and which was built by Ferdinand de Hohenberg. The central hall here, with its large

Schönbrunn Palace: Gloriette.

Schöner Brunner
Fountain.

Schönbrunn Palace:
the chapel.

Schönbrunn Palace:
the theatre.

Schönbrunn Palace: Emperor Franz Josef I's bedroom.

Schönbrunn Palace: Salon of the Millions.

windows formerly adorned with splendid panes, was often used for court banquets and receptions. From the terrace, reached by means of a spiral staircase, the visitor can enjoy the most beautiful panoramic views of Vienna.

The interior of the palace is decorated in sumptuous Rococo style. The salons of the Schönbrunn were for many years the splendid setting in which the life of the court took place. Outstanding among the chambers is the Great Hall, whose ceiling is decorated with frescoes by Guglielmi and from which hang magnificent glass lamps. It was here that formal court banquets took place, often with more than a hundred guests.

Other rooms of particular historic or artistic interest include Emperor Franz Josef's office, decorated with a portrait of Empress Elisabeth, dating back to 1863 and one of Emperor Franz Josef himself at the age of 30, both by Franz Russ, the Little Hall, decorated in 1761 by Albert Boller, the Salon of the Horses, featuring copper engravings by Johann Georg von Hamilton, the Napoleon Room, where the French emperor lived when Schönbrunn was converted into his headquarters between 1805 and 1809, the China Room, the Gobelins Room and the Red Room. The building on the east side of the palace, formerly the Schönbrunn winter riding school, now houses a coach and carriage museum, the largest of its type in the world, known as the **"Castle of Coaches"**, exhibiting 130 pieces ranging from the luxurious to the utilitarian.

Among the famous historic personalities living here in the Schöbrunn Palace were Emperor Josef I, Empress Maria Theresa, Leopold II, his son, Franz I and

The Empress Maria Theresa.

The Emperor Franz I.

Emperor Ferdinand I. Special mention should be afforded to Emperor Franz Josef and his wife Elisabeth, popularly known as ''Sissi''. The former was born on 18 August 1830 and died on 16 November 1916 in the midst of World War I. He worked for years in this palace, up to the end of his life, a life marked by tragedy. His wife was assassinated in 1898 and his son Rudolf, heir to the throne, committed suicide one year later in Mayerling Castle.

Schönbrunn Palace, at night.

Schönbrunn Palace: an imperial carriage in the Coach and Carriage Musuem.

The Parish Church, Grinzing.

GRINZING (19, Bezirk)

Grinzing is, without doubt, the best-known district of Döbling. Documents dating back as far as 1114 already make mention of ''Grinzigan'' and the area is today renowned all over the world as Vienna's typical Heurigenort, the home of its young, home-grown wine. The wine of Grinzing is most refreshing, but mischievous, quickly going to the head, which is why the Viennese do not usually drink it without previously having a good meal.

Many of the typical taverns (Heurigenlokalen) also serve ''Backhenderln'', Viennese roast chicken, and these traditional eating and drinking houses are filled with good cheer when the typical music is played, music which provides a pleasant escape from the dai-ly grind.

Grinzing, a village on the outskirts of Vienna, with its gardens and vineyards, still preserves many of its traditional old houses, along with its beautiful Late-Gothic parish church. A visit here, in the words of a well-known Viennese song, is sure to leave the tourist with pleasant memories and a promise to return soon. The history of wine-making is illustrated in the charming little wine museum of Grinzing.

Grinzing, «Heurigen».

Grinzing, Wine Museum.   *Grinzing, «Heurigen».*

THE HOUSE OF BEETHOVEN (19, Bezirk)

A wine-grower's house in Heiligenstadt achieved world fame when Beethoven stayed there in 1807, writing his celebrated Pastoral Symphony.

THE URANIA HOUSE (1, Uraniastrasse 1) was built by Max Fabiani between 1909 and 1910. In this ''teaching institution'' there is an observatory (in the dome of the building) and a cinema, as well as the installation where Vienna's mean time is electronically registered.

THE FEDERAL MINISTRY (''Oktoneum'', 3, Radetzkystrasse 2) was built in 1986 by P. Czernin and is the seat of the federal ministries and administration.

The monument to Johann Strauss, born in Vienna in 1825. The 496 works by this great composer include Die Fliedermaus, The Gypsy Baron, *and the universally-known waltz* The Blue Danube.

A panoramic view of the Danube Canal, the Franz Josef docks and Saint Stephen's Cathedral.

THE ROSSAU BARRACKS, also known as the Rodolfo Barracks, is a huge Windsor-style brick complex, constructed between 1865 and 1869 by Karl Pihal and Karl Markl. It stands on the banks of the Danube Canal, in the ninth district of the city, in Rossau.

When the first troops took up their station at these barracks, it was discovered that the architects had forgotten to install lavatory facilities.

THE DANUBE CANAL, approximately 17 kilometres in length, has constituted an adjustable stretch of the River Danube, separating the city centre from the second district, since its inauguration in 1598. A boat trip on its waters forms a highly pleasurable excursion.

THE ARSENAL (3, Arsenalstrasse)

The Arsenal was built between 1849 and 1856 by E. van der Null, Siccardsburg, Rösner, Rigel and Förster, according to the concept of defensive barracks which reigned after the revolution of 1848. A collection of 72 objects was formerly housed here, but the building and its contents were badly damaged during the Second World War.

The Rossauer
Barracks.

Danube Canal: the
floating restaurant
«Johann Strauss».

When the Imperial Bridge crossing the Danube collapsed in 1976, a new modern construction took its place.

The **Church of Saint Francis of Assisi,** also known as the ''Emperor Memorial Church'' (2, Mexicoplatz), was built between 1898 and 1913 to commemorate the 50th anniversary of the reign of Emperor Franz Josef I. Another interesting sight is the bridge over the Danube, one of the most impressive modern bridges in the world, built to replace the Imperial Bridge **(Reichsbrücke),** which collapsed in 1976.

Wiew of Danube and port of Vienna.

Uno city with Russian Church.

*The Vienna Islamic Centre (21, Am Hubertusdamm 17),
built in 1979 thanks to a donation from the king of Saudi
Arabia, Faisal Bin Abdul Aziz.*

Vienna's International Centre.

THE VIENNA INTERNATIONAL CENTRE, "UNO-CITY" (22 Bezirk), was built between 1973 and 1979 to the plans of the architect Johann Staber, and bestowed on the United Nations by the Republic of Austria on 23 August 1979. This act converted Vienna, already the scene for many international conferences and meetings, into the third UNO head-quarters, after New York and Geneva.

A view of Kahlenberg
and Leopoldsberg from
the Danube Tower.

Danube Tower.

Kahlenberg.

The Old Danube and the Danube Tower.

THE DANUBE PARK AND TOWER

In 1964, to mark the occasion of the Vienna Gardens Exhibition, the **Danube Park** (Donaupark) was constructed between the **Danube** and the **Old Danube**. This splendid recreational area also contains the 252 metre-high **Danube Tower**. On a clear day, marvellous views of the city may be obtained from the viewing balcony and revolving restaurant, situated 150 metres up this towering architectural prodigy.

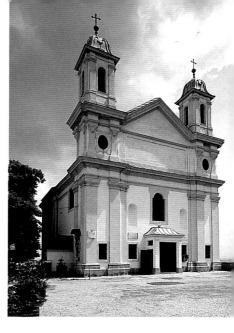

The Church of Saint Joseph, Kakhlenberg, with the Sobieski Chapel, commemorating the mass celebrated by the army of liberation before going into battle against the Turks.

KAHLENBERG AND LEOPOLDSBERG (19, Bezirk)

The Church of Saint Leopold in Leopoldsberg, completed in 1693, which stands on the mountain named after it.

These soaring summits encircling Vienna form the dying foothills of the Alps and from them can be seen on clear days a splendid panoramic view of the Danube and the Austrian capital. It was from these heights that the troops of the Polish **king Johann III Sobieski,** together with the Austrian army, launched the offensive which freed Vienna from the Turkish siege.

View of Kahlenberg and Leopoldsberg.

A boat-trip on Europe's largest subterranean lake.

"SEEGROTTE" (THE CAVE IN THE LAKE)
(Hinterbrühl bei Wien)

The Seegrotte is a subterranean marvel situated in Hinterbrühl, a locality near to Vienna in the south of the *Wienerwald,* the Vienna woods. It is a disused plaster mine from the last century which was flooded by 20 million litres of water in 1912 when cracks appeared in the walls of the cave, forcing the closure of the mine for economic reasons. The water was pumped out in 1932, revealing an underground lake measuring 6,200 square metres, the largest in Europe. Soon, motorboat excursions on the lake became popular, but in 1944 the water was pumped out again to convert the place into the factory where **the first jet fighter, the HE 162,** was built. Totally destroyed during the war, restoration work was carried out between 1945 and 1948, converting it once more into a major tourist attraction, open throughout the year.

This was where the first jet fighter, the Heinkel HE 162, was built.

MÖDLING (NE)

The Town Hall.

The Charnel House («Karner»).

Mödling, referred to in documents as far back as the year 907, has had the status of free city since 1875. Interesting among its mouments are the Renaissance-style town hall, built in 1548, the 12th-century Romanesque *Karner* (charnel house) and the Column of the Holy Trinity, with its magnificent stone sculptures.

The «Verdun Altar» at the Augustine Convent dates back to 1181, and is just one of teh many marvels waiting to greet the visitor to historic Vienna.

The collecgiate, Klosterneuburg.

Kreuzenstein Castle.

Veste Liechenstein.

KLOSTERNEUBERG (NE)

This tiny wine-growing city, lying at the foot of Mount Kahlenberg, historic residence of the Babenbergs and burial-place of the patron saint of the area, Saint Leopold, owes its cultural and economic importance to the Augustine convent founded here in 1100.

KREUZENSTEIN CASTLE (NE)

To the north-east of Korneuburg rises the impressive outline of Kreuzenstein Castle. Documents referring to it as the property of Formbacher date back to 1115, but the castle was destroyed in 1645. It was built up again from its ruins by **Hans Graf Wilczek**, who converted it into the medieval castle of one's dreams. The buildings contain interesting collections of armour, *objets d'art* and a fine library.

Heiligenkreuz Collegiate.

VESTE LIECHENSTEIN
(Maria Enzerdorf, NE)

This is the 12th-century Romanesque castle *par excellence*. During the passing of time, it suffered serious damage, the worst at the hands of the Turks in 1683. Restoration work began in 1808, by order of Johann I of Liechenstein, and by 1873 the castle had wholly regained its impressive Romanesque appearance.

HEILIGENKREUZ MONASTERY (NE)

The beautiful Cistercian Monastery of the Holy Cross was built in 1133 by Leopold the Holy. The interior courtyard contains two masterpieces by Giovanni Giuliani, the *Column of the Trinity* and the *Fountain of Saint Joseph*. The transept, supported by 300 marble columns, was built between 1220 and 1250.

Laxenburg, Franzensburg.

The former Laxenburg Palace.

LAXENBURG PALACE (NE)

This palace, acquired by the House of Hapsburg in the 14th century, was primarily used as a hunting pavilion, and was later restored, converted into a Baroque-style building which was used as a holiday residence. In 1798, Emperor Franz I ordered the **Franzenburg** Castle built on an island in the centre of the huge park, a classical Romantic edifice which was completed in 1836. Architectural elements from castles, churches and convents of various periods were used in the construction of magnificent creation.